# Silent Words Loudly Spoken

Church Sign Sayings

## David J. Claassen

CSS Publishing Company, Inc., Lima, Ohio

SILENT WORDS LOUDLY SPOKEN

Copyright © 2005 by
CSS Publishing Company, Inc.
Lima, Ohio

All rights reserved. No part of this publication may be reproduced in any manner whatsoever without the prior permission of the publisher, except in the case of brief quotations embodied in critical articles and reviews. Inquiries should be addressed to: Permissions, CSS Publishing Company, Inc., P.O. Box 4503, Lima, Ohio 45802-4503.

**Library of Congress Cataloging-in-Publication Data**

Silent words loudly spoken : church sign sayings / [compiled by] David J. Claassen.
   p. cm.
   ISBN 0-87880-2342-X (perfect bound : alk. paper)
1. Church signs. I. Claassen, Dav id J., 1950- II. Title

BV653.7.S55 2004
254'.3—dc22

2004026370

For more information about CSS Publishing Company resources, visit our website at www.csspub.com or e-mail us at custserv@csspub.com or call (800) 241-4056.

Cover design by Chris Patton
ISBN 0-7880-2342-X

PRINTED IN U.S.A.

*Dedicated
to the three men
who, over the years,
have acted
as signkeeper
at the church I serve*

*(The late) Bernie Rachuba
Ralph Overholt
and
Dennis Haynes*

*Thanks
for helping us
proclaim a
silent message
loudly spoken!*

# Table Of Contents

| | |
|---|---|
| Introduction | 7 |
| Ten Commandments Of A Good Church Sign | 9 |
| The Effective Church Sign | 11 |
| Christmas | 17 |
| Holy Week | 21 |
| Thanksgiving | 25 |
| General | 29 |

# Introduction

Thousands of cars drive by your church every day. What do the occupants of those cars see as they pass your church property? They see your church facility, but there's something in front of your church that catches their eye, or should. It's your church's sign. What an opportunity, a congregation of thousands passing by each and every day! Don't panic. You can have fresh and inspiring messages for that sign each week. The sayings in this book will give you two fresh statements, one for each side of your sign, for seven years (assuming you'll take a few weeks each year to promote events of interest to the public).

The majority of the sayings are edited and paraphrased from my readings over the years. A few came to me from "sign scouts" in my church who saw a sign that grabbed their attention in front of some church somewhere. Several are verbatim quotes of a Christian giant of the past, but I'm sure they wouldn't mind. A number have undoubtedly made the rounds, but I've tried to stay away from the tried, true, but tiring sayings we've all seen.

Each phrase contains no more than eighteen letters and spaces per line and they fit on three lines. Jot down the date beside the phrase when you use it.

May God use your church sign as an effective ministry tool. It's your pulpit out on the front lawn, proclaiming silent words loudly spoken!

# Ten Commandments
# Of A Good Church Sign

1. Thou shalt not use so many words that it's impossible to read the entire message when traveling ten miles per hour over the speed limit, the slowest anyone will drive.

2. Thou shalt use large enough letters so they can be read easily from the road on a foggy night by a driver who has a burned out headlight.

3. Thou shalt not keep the same message in the sign for weeks on end, giving the impression that nobody's minding the church.

4. Thou shalt not leave a time-dated message on the sign more than a day after the event or holiday. You might as well put "we can't keep up with the times" on your sign.

5. Thou shalt use different messages on each side of the sign so people get into the habit of reading it both coming and going.

6. Thou shalt keep the message positive. Who wants to be scolded by a sign? A negative message, no matter how true, when given without the benefit of the human touch of love, will be rejected anyway.

7. Thou shalt not leave the sign empty, for this communicates you have nothing to say and have said it clearly.

8. Thou shalt use thought-provoking messages that leave the reader pondering.

9. Thou shalt not promote "in house" programs of no interest to the average person driving or walking by. John Q. Public couldn't care less that the Right Reverend I.M. Boring is going to be the guest preacher next Sunday.

10. Thou shalt not use "thou" and other "in house" religious terms on your sign.

# The Effective Church Sign

"Gotcha!" the billboard stated in big bold letters. In much smaller print were the words "Caught you reading billboards again." The billboard company wanted to remind potential advertisers that people read those big signs. (Many companies already know this and spend large numbers of advertising dollars on billboard messages.)

Churches don't have to rent billboards. They can own a smaller but effective version: a well-designed church sign with interchangeable letters. The following checklist can guide leaders in that endeavor.

**Placement.** A new sign must meet the community's sign code requirements. Choose a reputable sign company familiar with the local code — which usually limits a sign's size, height, and distance from the street. The property's zoning around the church will also affect the requirements. Your pre-existing signs, such as the church name affixed to the church building or a sign advertising day care, can also affect approval of a new church sign. Most codes limit the number of signs you can have.

Working within the guidelines of the local code, place the sign in a location that makes it most visible from the road. It should be near enough to your building that people know it goes with your church.

**Lighting.** In most cases, you will want the sign illuminated. Timers or sunlight-driven photoelectric cells can ensure that energy is not wasted on daytime illumination. In the winter months be sure to have the sign lighted during the busy drive times of dawn and dusk.

**Lettering.** Two common mistakes: (a) lettering that is too small and (b) trying to cram too much information on the sign. This applies to both the church name portion of the sign and the changeable letter section. Note the average speed the traffic travels by the sign and its distance from the road. The entire message should be readable in the time it takes a driver to go by.

Carefully choose colors for both background and letters. A color combination may be attractive, but the colors must also work together to make the sign as legible as possible.

**Purpose.** Is the purpose of your sign to inform parishioners or non-attenders? In most situations more non-attenders than attenders will see the sign. Use the Sunday bulletin, the church newsletter, announcement time in worship, and in-house bulletin boards to communicate with parishioners. Use the church sign to communicate with non-attenders.

**Procedures.** Determine what kind of information you wish to communicate with the non-attenders. Some good rules:

1. Advertise only church events likely to draw non-attenders. This might include special Easter or Christmas services or cantatas, or perhaps a fund-raising event open to the public. You would not advertise a Sunday school teacher appreciation dinner or a service of baptism. These events do not generally interest non-attenders.

2. Change the message frequently, at least once a week. People develop the habit of looking at a sign if they know it regularly displays a new message.

3. Use a different message on each side of the sign. Most people take the same route going to and from their destination and read both sides of the sign. This doubles the number of messages communicated.

4. Give the gift of a thoughtful message. People enjoy an inspirational phrase or a statement that makes them think. Stay away from negative messages or statements that are too preachy. Some of the best ideas can come from your own personal reading. Jot down phrases that you can shorten and adapt to your sign's limited space. Our church's leaders often hear people say that they drive out of their way to see what is on our church sign. Occasionally, a visitor attends worship because some of the messages were especially meaningful.

5. Advertising church events sparingly and keeping the majority of the messages inspirational make the occasional church-activity advertisement more effective. People find signs that give them something more attractive rather than signs that ask for a response.

6. Identify one person who can change the sign on a regular basis. Changing the lettering in inclement weather requires substantial dedication. That person must therefore understand the signkeeper ministry's importance. As with any volunteer position, regularly affirm the ministry. Make certain that positive comments about the sign are communicated to the signkeeper.

A well-designed church sign is a major investment, but worth the cost if wisely utilized. The church sign offers your first chance to communicate with people who drive or walk by your church. A well-utilized sign gives a great first impression of your church and reaches out to those who have not yet attended your services.

---

Editor's note: This was originally published in *Net Results* (Lubbock, Texas: Net Results, Inc., August 1997), www.netresults.org. Used by permission.

# Christmas

**Notes/Dates Used**

JESUS CAME TO
EARTH SO WE COULD
GO TO HEAVEN


CHRIST IS GOD'S
LOVE GIFT WRAPPED
IN HUMAN FLESH


XMAS IGNORES HIM
WHO MAKES THE
SEASON POSSIBLE


WHAT GOD WANTS
FOR CHRISTMAS
IS YOU


JESUS CAME TO
US SO THAT WE
MIGHT COME TO HIM


TODAY IS A GIFT,
THAT'S WHY IT'S
THE PRESENT

# Holy Week

**Notes/Dates Used**

JESUS' DEATH
CAN GIVE
US LIFE

HOW ODD OF
GOD TO
CHOOSE US

JESUS' PAIN
IS
OUR GAIN

IT COST GOD MORE
TO SAVE OUR WORLD
THAN TO CREATE IT

JESUS CHANGED
DEATH FROM A DEAD
END TO A DOORWAY

THE RESURRECTION
OF JESUS ISN'T
RUMOR, IT'S FACT

BECAUSE JESUS
LIVES WE HAVE THE
HOPE OF HEAVEN

**Notes/Dates Used**

THE EMPTY TOMB
MEANS WE CAN
HAVE A FULL LIFE

# Thanksgiving

                                                    **Notes/Dates Used**

ADOPT AN
ATTITUDE
OF GRATITUDE


THINK OF FIVE
REASONS WHY YOU
CAN GIVE THANKS


THANKSGIVING
LEADS TO
THANKS-LIVING


TO REJOICE
IS A
CHOICE


IF WE PAUSE TO
THINK WE'LL HAVE
CAUSE TO THANK


BE THANKFUL YOU
DON'T GET WHAT
YOU DESERVE


BE THANKFUL YOU
GET WHAT YOU
DON'T DESERVE

# General

**Notes/Dates Used**

DON'T FOCUS ON
YOUR PROBLEM BUT
ON GOD'S POWER


GOD GOES
WITH YOU
EVERYWHERE


MANAGE YOUR TIME
AND YOU
MANAGE YOURSELF


PATIENCE
CARRIES A LOT OF
WAIT


HAPPINESS
IS AN
INSIDE JOB


IF YOU CAN'T PAY
SOMEONE BACK,
PAY IT FORWARD


HUMILITY IS
SEEING OURSELVES
AS GOD SEES US

**Notes/Dates Used**

COME ON OVER
AND BRING
THE KIDS

PRAYER HAS
NO ROAMING
CHARGES

THERE IS A GOD,
AND WE'RE
NOT HIM

THOUGHTS
EVENTUALLY HAVE
CONSEQUENCES

GOD'S GREATEST
GIFT IN PRAYER
IS HIMSELF

NO SIN EVER
LIVES UP TO
ITS PROMISE

THOUGHTS, WORDS,
AND PRAYER ARE
LIKE SEEDS

Notes/Dates Used

BE PART OF GOD'S
CONSPIRACY TO
UNDERMINE EVIL


YOU'RE NEVER
A LOSER
UNTIL YOU QUIT


DON'T WAIT TO
UNDERSTAND BEFORE
YOU BELIEVE


CONSIDER GOD'S
FRIENDSHIP YOUR
HIGHEST PRIORITY


WE GET TO KNOW
GOD BY LEARNING
TO BE OBEDIENT


WISHING AND
PLANNING TAKE
THE SAME ENERGY


THERE IS MORE OF
THE GOODNESS OF
GOD TO KNOW

**Notes/Dates Used**

BREAK A BAD
HABIT BY
DROPPING IT

GOD WANTS
YOUR COMPLETE
ATTENTION

SEE GOD AS MORE
THAN YOUR
NEED-MEETER

GOD HELPS IN
PROPORTION TO
OUR PROBLEMS

DON'T LET
YESTERDAY
USE UP TODAY

MAKE AN EFFORT
NOT
AN EXCUSE

GOD'S LOVE
WILL NOT
LET YOU GO

**Notes/Dates Used**

FAITH ATTEMPTS
GREAT THINGS
FOR GOD

FAITH EXPECTS
GREAT THINGS
FROM GOD

DETERMINE TO
WANT WHAT
GOD WANTS

DON'T WASTE
YOUR FAILURES,
LEARN FROM THEM

STRANGERS ARE
FRIENDS WAITING
TO HAPPEN

LET YOURSELF
BE FOUND
BY GOD

GOD HAS MADE US
RESTLESS UNTIL
WE REST IN HIM

**Notes/Dates Used**

TALK IS CHEAP
BECAUSE SUPPLY
EXCEEDS DEMAND


GOD IS NOT
LIMITED BY YOUR
LIMITATIONS


LET GOD DO
WITH YOU AS
HE PLEASES


PRAY BECAUSE
GOD IS
RESOURCEFUL


GOD HAS A
SURPRISE FOR YOU.
WATCH FOR IT


GOD DOESN'T
CAUSE OUR PAIN
BUT HE CAN USE IT


GOD PAYS
ATTENTION
TO YOU

**Notes/Dates Used**

THE GLORY OF GOD
IS A PERSON
FULLY ALIVE


GOD USES
OUR WAITING
TO HELP US GROW


PEOPLE KNOW WE
HAVE A HEART WHEN
WE GIVE A HAND


GOD CANNOT LOVE
US MORE AND WILL
NOT LOVE US LESS


THE MOUTH IS
OFTEN OPENED
BY MISTAKE


GOD IS
OUT TO DO
YOU GOOD


A LIE HAS SPEED,
TRUTH HAS
ENDURANCE

**Notes/Dates Used**

ONLY A FAITH THAT
IS COSTLY ENDS UP
BEING VALUABLE

GOD CAN ONLY
FILL AN
UPTURNED HEART

IT'S NOT OUTLOOK
THAT COUNTS,
BUT UPLOOK

GOD OFTEN LEADS
US ON THE
ROUNDABOUT WAY

GOD'S LOVE WILL
CHANGE YOU
FOR THE BETTER

WE ARE BORN
BROKEN. GOD'S
GRACE IS OUR GLUE

SPIRITUAL
A.D.D.
TREATED HERE

Notes/Dates Used

QUIET YOUR NOISY
DESIRES ENOUGH
TO HEAR FROM GOD


GIVE UP WHAT
WILL TAKE
YOU DOWN


SEE WHAT JESUS
WOULD IF LOOKING
THROUGH YOUR EYES


DO THE WORK OF
GOD BY GIVING
PEOPLE ATTENTION


ABILITY ISN'T AS
IMPORTANT TO GOD
AS AVAILABILITY


THE BIGGEST GAP
IS BETWEEN "I
SHOULD" & "I DID"


GOD IS COMPETENT
TO LEAD.
LET HIM LEAD

**Notes/Dates Used**

FAULTS ARE
THICK WHERE
LOVE IS THIN


HAVE A GREAT DAY,
OR DO YOU HAVE
OTHER PLANS?


A DIAMOND IS COAL
MADE GOOD
UNDER PRESSURE


GRUDGES ARE LIKE
BABIES. THEY ONLY
GROW BY NURSING


GIVE YOURSELF TO
OTHERS & YOU'LL
FIND YOURSELF


ACCEPT THE
RESPONSIBILITIES
GOD GIVES


FORWARD MOMENTUM
IS BETTER THAN
BACKWARD MOMENTUM

**Notes/Dates Used**

FORGIVING SETS US
MORE FREE THAN
THE ONE FORGIVEN


BE GENEROUS WITH
YOUR LIFE & IT
WILL BE FULL


SOMETIMES THE
GREATEST RISK IS
IN DOING NOTHING


ALWAYS ADD
PRAYER TO
YOUR TEARS


PRAY ABOUT YOUR
DOUBTS. GOD
WON'T GET MAD


LIFE IS FRAGILE.
HANDLE WITH
PRAYER


START THE DAY
RIGHT. MEET
WITH GOD FIRST

**Notes/Dates Used**

FAITH TURNS
SEALED CAVES INTO
OPEN TUNNELS


GOD CAN'T FILL
SOMEONE WHO'S
FULL OF SELF


HAVE RECKLESS
RELIANCE
ON GOD


BELIEVING
IS
SEEING


SUPERIOR JOY
COMES FROM
JESUS CHRIST


PURSUE HAPPINESS
BY DRAWING
CLOSE TO GOD


AIM FOR GOD TO
BE YOUR GREATEST
SATISFACTION

**Notes/Dates Used**

A CRISIS IS AN
OPPORTUNITY
FOR CHANGE


IT COSTS TO OBEY
GOD, BUT IT
COSTS MORE NOT TO


WE CAN TRIP OVER
FAILURE OR
BUILD ON IT


THE DARKEST HOUR
IS ONLY 60
MINUTES LONG


BEWARE OF BRIEF
DELIGHT AND
LASTING SHAME


EXPECT
THE
UNEXPECTED


A HALF TRUTH
IS A
WHOLE LIE

**Notes/Dates Used**

WHEN YOU
FAIL,
FAIL FORWARD


BEGIN WITH
THE END
IN MIND


A MARRIAGE
LICENSE IS A
LEARNER'S PERMIT


GOD HAS YOUR
BEST INTERESTS
AT HEART


GUILT IS GOOD IF
IT TURNS US TO
GOD'S FORGIVENESS


LIFE'S TRINKETS
DISTRACT US
FROM GOD'S GOLD


GOD IS DOING MORE
IN YOUR LIFE THAN
YOU NOW SEE

**Notes/Dates Used**

WHEN GOD HOLDS US
SUFFERING CAN'T
DESTROY US


EACH DAY IS
PACKED WITH
POSSIBILITIES


THE BEST THINGS
IN LIFE
AREN'T THINGS


GOD CAN USE OUR
PAST PAIN FOR
FUTURE GAIN


BE ALERT TO WHAT
GOD IS DOING WITH
WHAT'S HAPPENING


WEAK PEOPLE HAVE
WISHES. GREAT
PEOPLE HAVE WILLS


GOD CAN USE
EVERYTHING THAT'S
GOING ON WITH YOU

**Notes/Dates Used**

SEE POSSIBILITIES
BEFORE THEY
BECOME OBVIOUS


FEAR CAN'T
CO-EXIST WITH
FAITH


GET IN THE HABIT
OF THINKING GREAT
THOUGHTS OF GOD


BE FAITHFUL TO
GOD'S TASK
AT HAND


WE MAKE DECISIONS
AND OUR DECISIONS
MAKE US


EVERY EVENT HAS
GOD'S PURPOSE
BEHIND IT


YOU CAN'T HURRY
WAITING
FOR GOD

**Notes/Dates Used**

GOD'S TIMING MAY
NOT BE OURS, BUT
IT'S ALWAYS RIGHT


FORBIDDEN FRUIT
CREATES
MANY JAMS


THE WORLD IS
CHARGED WITH THE
GRANDEUR OF GOD


GOD IS AT WORK
IN THE WORST
OF CIRCUMSTANCES


LITTLE GOOD IS
DONE BY ACTING
OUT OF IMPATIENCE


YOUR CALLING FROM
GOD IS TO BE
YOUR COMPASS


WATCH FOR A GIFT
GOD WILL GIVE
YOU TODAY

**Notes/Dates Used**

WE'RE NEVER
BEYOND THE REACH
OF GOD'S HAND

STARTING WELL IS
EASY. ENDING WELL
TAKES ENDURANCE

PRAY FOR A GOOD
HARVEST BUT
CONTINUE TO HOE

A SMILE IS THE
SAME IN ANY
LANGUAGE

DREAMS BECOME
REALITY THROUGH
PERSEVERANCE

FOLLOW GOD'S
AGENDA FOR
TODAY

OUR WEAKNESS
LETS GOD REVEAL
HIS STRENGTH

**Notes/Dates Used**

HAVE CONFIDENCE
IN GOD'S
RELIABILITY


EGO STANDS
FOR
"EDGING GOD OUT"


PRAY BECAUSE
GOD IS
RESOURCEFUL


WITH GOD WE ARE
NOT A STATISTIC,
WE HAVE STATUS


WHEN TROUBLES COME
DESIRE GOD
MORE THAN ANSWERS


GOD'S GRACE MEANS
HE WILL ALWAYS BE
THERE FOR YOU


FRIENDSHIP WITH
GOD CAN DEEPEN
IN TOUGH TIMES

**Notes/Dates Used**

DESIRE GOD
HIMSELF, NOT JUST
WHAT HE CAN GIVE


WHEN PEOPLE PLAY
GOD THEY ACT
LIKE THE DEVIL


GOD HAS CREATED
US FOR FRIENDSHIP
WITH HIM


QUIET YOUR MIND
AND SOUL ENOUGH TO
HEAR GOD WHISPER


GOD USES OUR
WAITING TO
HELP US GROW


GOD WILL BE
PRESENT WHERE
HE IS WANTED


WE'RE NOT SMART
ENOUGH FOR GOD TO
GIVE US ALL WE ASK

**Notes/Dates Used**

FAITH MAKES
A GOOD
PILLOW


FRIENDSHIP WITH
GOD PAYS MORE
THAN IT COSTS


PRAYER IS ONE
WAY GOD LETS US
CHANGE OUR WORLD


"I DON'T QUESTION
YOUR EXISTENCE"
         — GOD


EVERYTHING THAT
HAPPENS, GOD IS
PREPARED TO USE


OUR LIMITATIONS
HAVE THEIR
LIMITS


ACCEPT NO
SUBSTITUTE
FOR GOD

**Notes/Dates Used**

WITH GOD'S HELP
YOU CAN BECOME
YOURSELF

CIRCUMSTANCES ARE
NOT IN CONTROL OF
YOUR CHARACTER

DOMINATED BY
SELF? BECOME
OBEDIENT TO GOD

HEROIC DEFEATS
CAN RIVAL
VICTORIES

DQ ISN'T THE
ONLY PLACE WITH
GREAT SUNDAYS

SEVEN DAYS
WITHOUT PRAYER
MAKE ONE WEAK

WE DON'T FIND GOD
WE LET OURSELVES
BE FOUND

**Notes/Dates Used**

BE MORE SURE
OF GOD THAN YOU
ARE OF YOURSELF


SUCCESS IS DOING
THE NEXT THING
WELL


MAKE EVERY
PLEASURE A REASON
TO PRAISE GOD


THE ESSENCE OF
GENIUS IS KNOWING
WHAT TO OVERLOOK


NEVER LIVE AS
THOUGH GOD
DOES NOT EXIST


EARTH HAS NO
SORROW THAT
HEAVEN CAN'T HEAL


WE PREACH A
MESSAGE OF THE
SECOND CHANCE

**Notes/Dates Used**

GOD ALWAYS HAS
FRESH WAYS TO
SHOW YOU HIS LOVE

MAKING NO CHOICE
IS THE SAME AS
A WRONG CHOICE

TRUST AN UNKNOWN
FUTURE TO A
KNOWING GOD

IT SADDENS GOD
WHEN WE DOUBT
HIS LOVE FOR US

FEED YOUR FAITH
AND YOUR DOUBTS
WILL STARVE

YOU'LL SMILE
BETTER IF YOU
GET A FAITH LIFT

THE TONGUE WEIGHS
LITTLE BUT FEW
CAN HOLD IT

**Notes/Dates Used**

THE GREATEST
VICTORY TO WIN
IS OVER SELF


TIME CAN BE
WASTED, BUT
NEVER RECYCLED


WHAT IS WORSE
THAN FALLING IS
TO REMAIN FALLEN


SUCCESS IS SWEET
BUT ITS
SECRET IS SWEAT


TO BE LOVED,
BE
LOVABLE


THE WEAK CAN'T
FORGIVE ...
ONLY THE STRONG


WHAT GOD CALLS
US TO HE
EQUIPS US FOR

**Notes/Dates Used**

FAITH IS TAKING A
STEP IN THE FACE
OF UNCERTAINTY


TO BE HIGHLY
ESTEEMED BY
GOD, BE HUMBLE


JOIN US AS WE
CONSIDER WHAT'S
ON GOD'S MIND


IS YOUR BACK OR
YOUR FACE
TOWARD GOD?


FIND CHRIST AND
YOU'LL DISCOVER
YOUR TRUE SELF


GOD CAN'T HELP
THE
SELF-RELIANT


GOD'S GIFTS
ARE OURS
FOR OTHERS

**Notes/Dates Used**

WHEN LIFE IS LESS
THAN IDEAL, GOD
CAN BE MOST REAL

GOD YEARNS TO
BE HEARD AS
WELL AS TO HEAR

WELL DONE IS
BETTER THAN
WELL SAID

YOU ARE GOD'S
ANSWER TO
SOMEONE'S PRAYER

HOT WORDS MAKE
FOR COOL
RELATIONSHIPS

WHEN WE PRAY,
"COINCIDENCES"
HAPPEN MORE OFTEN

THE CHILD'S
FIRST SCHOOL IS
THE FAMILY

CHARACTER IS
AN ACHIEVEMENT,
NOT A GIFT

BETTER THAN BEING
ABOVE US, GOD
CAN BE IN US

WE DON'T JUMP
TO FAILURE, WE
INCH TOWARD IT

FAITH TRUSTS
ENOUGH TO
WAIT

A COMPLIMENT
FROM ANOTHER IS
A GIFT FROM GOD

NO DAY
IS
INSIGNIFICANT

FORGET WHAT
CHRIST HAS
FORGIVEN

**Notes/Dates Used**

JOIN US SUNDAY.
WE'RE PLANNING ON
GOD SHOWING UP


WE HAVE CONQUERED
OUTER SPACE BUT
NOT INNER SPACE


WEALTH IS WHAT
YOU HAVE THAT YOU
WOULD NEVER SELL


WHEN WE START
GIVING WE
START LIVING


DIFFICULTIES
ARE DOORS
TO GROWTH


THIS CHURCH IS A
CLINIC SERVED BY
DR. JESUS


GOD IS
TOO WISE
TO BE WRONG

**Notes/Dates Used**

GOD IS TOO
GOOD TO BE
UNKIND


WE DON'T GET MUCH
DONE BY
STARTING TOMORROW


DON'T TRY TO LIVE
MORE THAN ONE
DAY AT A TIME


YOU ARE IMMORTAL
UNTIL GOD'S WORK
FOR YOU IS DONE


THE FUTURE
IS NOT
BEHIND YOU


WE CAN TURN FROM
GOD'S LOVE BUT
WE CAN'T STOP IT


GOD IS
DETERMINED
TO LOVE YOU

Notes/Dates Used

WANTS AND
NEEDS ARE
NOT THE SAME


"DELIGHT YOURSELF
IN THE LORD"
PSALM 37:4


REMEMBERED
JOYS
ARE NEVER PAST


GOD IS ALWAYS
UP TO SOMETHING
GOOD IN YOUR LIFE


LIVE YOUR LIFE
AS IF JESUS WERE
IN YOUR PLACE


JOY IS J-ESUS,
O-THERS, THEN
Y-OURSELF


WORRY IS
MISUSED
IMAGINATION

**Notes/Dates Used**

TO HAVE A GOOD
IDEA, HAVE LOTS
OF IDEAS


BE SALT & LIGHT,
THEN
SHAKE & SHINE


BE A PIPELINE OF
GOODNESS. LET
GOD BE THE PUMP


GOOD HABITS CAN
OVERCOME
BAD HABITS


LOVE IS
SPELLED
T-I-M-E


GOD EMPTIES US
OF SELF TO GIVE
MORE ROOM FOR HIM


DO UNTO OTHERS
AS THOUGH YOU
WERE OTHERS

**Notes/Dates Used**

A SMOOTH SEA
NEVER MADE A
SKILLFUL SAILOR


BE MASTERED BY
CHRIST & YOU'LL
MASTER LIFE


BE THANKFUL FOR
STUMBLES; THEY
CAN PREVENT FALLS


IF YOU WOULDN'T
WRITE IT & SIGN
IT, DON'T SAY IT


WAITING IS
A GREAT
TEACHER


TO BE HAPPY,
MAKE OTHERS
HAPPY


LIFE IS TOO SHORT
TO BE
LIVED SMALL

Notes/Dates Used

THERE IS ALWAYS
TIME TO DO
THE WILL OF GOD

JOIN US SUNDAY
AND RECOVER AN
AWARENESS OF GOD

GOD REALLY WANTS
TO BE
GOOD TO YOU

DON'T FIX THE
BLAME. FIX
THE PROBLEM

RECEIVE GOD'S
GIFT OF
GUILT REMOVED

GOD KNOWS YOU
BETTER THAN YOU
KNOW YOURSELF

QUIT HUGGING THE
TRUNK. GET OUT
ON A LIMB

**Notes/Dates Used**

COMMITMENT IS
ANOTHER NAME
FOR SUCCESS

TRUTH EXISTS
WHETHER WE
SEE IT OR NOT

PATIENCE IS
RESPECTING GOD'S
TIMETABLE

WE SHOULD
LISTEN AS WELL
AS WE HEAR

ONLY THE
DISCIPLINED
ARE FREE

ORGANIZE LIFE
AROUND FAITH,
NOT FEAR

GIVE UP ON
SELF & GIVE
SELF UP TO GOD

**Notes/Dates Used**

INCREASE YOUR
CAPACITY
TO ENJOY GOD


GOD FINDS
PLEASURE IN YOUR
LOVE FOR HIM


WHEN PRAISED,
TAKE IT WITH A
GRAIN OF SALT


WHEN CRITICIZED,
LOOK FOR THE
GRAIN OF TRUTH


DIAMONDS ARE MADE
UNDER PRESSURE.
SO ARE SAINTS


ARE WE A GUEST
WHO TAKES OR A
HOST WHO GIVES?


WE DON'T KNOW
A TRUTH UNTIL
WE APPLY IT

**Notes/Dates Used**

WE CANNOT BE
BOTH HUMBLE AND
PROUD OF IT

TREAT YOUR
FAMILY
LIKE GUESTS

TREAT YOUR
GUESTS
LIKE FAMILY

GOD GIVES US GOOD
THINGS IN SPITE
OF OURSELVES

TODAY IS
A UNIQUE
EVENT

DON'T DEMEAN YOUR
OWN UNIQUENESS BY
ENVYING OTHERS

TEMPTATION'S
PROMISE IS
A LIE

**Notes/Dates Used**

GIVE UP A PRAYER
TO GOD AND
GIVE UP ON WORRY


IT'S DANGEROUS
TO BE OUTSIDE
THE WILL OF GOD


MAKE GOD THE
SUPREME HUNGER
OF YOUR HEART


LIFE IS WHAT
HAPPENS WHILE
WE MAKE PLANS


LISTEN TO
GOD'S WHISPER
TODAY


WHEN A FRIEND
CRIES WE SHOULD
TASTE SALT


THE LESSONS OF
LIFE ARE READ
BACKWARD

**Notes/Dates Used**

WHAT HAS BECOME
CLEAR TO
YOU LATELY?


FAILING WELL IS
BETTER THAN
SUCCEEDING BADLY


WE ALL BECOME
LIKE WHAT
WE WORSHIP


REPLACE "HAVE TO
DO" WITH "WILLING
TO DO"


THE MILK OF HUMAN
KINDNESS HAS NO
EXPIRATION DATE


NO DAY
IS EMPTY OF
GOD'S PRESENCE


A LIFE STUFFED
WITH THINGS LACKS
A HUNGER FOR GOD

**Notes/Dates Used**

HAPPY HOUR(S)
AT
(your service time[s])


JOY & JESUS
COME INTO OUR
HEARTS TOGETHER


IT'S NOT WHAT YOU
OWN THAT COUNTS,
IT'S WHAT OWNS YOU


THE ONLY PEOPLE
WHO LIKE CHANGE
ARE WET BABIES


GOSSIP: THE MORE
INTERESTING, THE
LESS LIKELY TRUE


BOREDOM IS THE
CURSE OF
EMPTY PEOPLE


FEELING BETTER IS
NOT AS IMPORTANT
AS FINDING GOD

**Notes/Dates Used**

GOD HUMBLES
US INTO
GREATNESS

LIVE WITH YOUR
DESTINATION
IN VIEW

TRUST YOURSELF
LESS AND
GOD MORE

TO THINK
YOURSELF HUMBLE
IS TO LOSE IT

WE CAN PLANT AND
WATER, BUT GOD
MAKES THINGS GROW

GOD'S REALLY GOD.
HE'S NOT APPLYING
FOR THE JOB

GOD ALWAYS
HAS ANOTHER
MOVE

**Notes/Dates Used**

HABITS CAN BE
EITHER SERVANTS
OR MASTERS


KNOWING & NOT
DOING IS
NOT KNOWING


MAY YOUR DOING
GROW OUT
OF YOUR BEING


YOU CAN ONLY
SEE THE STARS
WHEN IT'S DARK


WHEN YOU FAIL
GOD LOVES YOU
JUST THE SAME


HERE AT CHURCH
GOD FIXES
DAMAGED PEOPLE


MOST OF
OUR WORRIES
NEVER HAPPEN

Notes/Dates Used

LIFE'S HEAVIEST
BURDEN IS HAVING
NOTHING TO CARRY

NEVER CEASE BEING
AMAZED BY GOD'S
FORGIVENESS

JESUS IS HEAT
FOR A COLD HEART
AT NO CHARGE

THE GREAT
PHYSICIAN HEALS
HEARTS HERE

BE PREOCCUPIED
WITH THOUGHTS OF
GOD TODAY

MAKE A BEAUTIFUL
ENDING OUT OF
A BAD BEGINNING

GOD DOESN'T TWIST
ARMS. HE HOLDS
OUT HIS HANDS

**Notes/Dates Used**

GOD'S RESTRAINT
IN OUR LIVES
GIVES US FREEDOM

HARBORING SIN
LIMITS
INTIMACY WITH GOD

PRIDE IS
A GOOD PILL
TO SWALLOW

GOD PACKS LIFE
WITH SURPRISES
ALL THE TIME

AN ATHEIST HAS
NO INVISIBLE
MEANS OF SUPPORT

GOD'S PLANS FOR
US ARE BETTER
THAN OUR OWN

PATIENCE IS
TRUSTING IN
GOD'S TIMING

**Notes/Dates Used**

FAITH & WORRY ARE
AS INCOMPATIBLE
AS OIL & WATER

A SHORTCUT IS
OFTEN TEMPTATION
IN DISGUISE

GOD DOES NOT GIVE
US TIME IN WHICH
TO DO NOTHING

GOD ANSWERS
PRAYER WITH
YES, NO, OR WAIT

DUSTY BIBLES
LEAD TO
DIRTY LIVES

THE GREATEST SIN
IS NOT TAKING
SIN SERIOUSLY

THE BEST ANTIQUE
IS AN
OLD FRIEND

**Notes/Dates Used**

WHEN YOU FIND
JESUS, YOU
FIND YOURSELF

FORGIVENESS GIVES
UP THE RIGHT TO
HURT OTHERS BACK

WE "GET LIFE"
ONE CHOICE
AT A TIME

YOU ARE GOING TO
BE WHAT YOU ARE
NOW BECOMING

MIGHTY SHOVES
MOVE LESS THAN
LITTLE PUSHES

ADOPT GOD'S
PURPOSES AS
YOUR OWN

THE BEAUTY OF
NATURE IS GOD'S
GREETING CARD

**Notes/Dates Used**

PROBLEMS ARE
OPPORTUNITIES
IN DISGUISE

TODAY YOU WRITE
ANOTHER PAGE IN
YOUR STORY

THIS CHURCH CAN
BE A SAFE
PLACE FOR YOU

IT'S EASIER TO
DEBATE THE BIBLE
THAN TO OBEY IT

LIVE SO AS TO
GET THE APPLAUSE
OF HEAVEN

OPPORTUNITY IS
OFTEN DISGUISED
AS WORK

GOD DOESN'T NEED
OUR ADVICE, JUST
OUR OBEDIENCE

Notes/Dates Used

WINDOWS ARE TO
LOOK THROUGH. SO
ARE YOUR PROBLEMS

GOD'S MERCY IS
GREATER THAN OUR
GREATEST SIN

COURAGE MEANS
DOING WHAT YOU
FEAR ANYWAY

LAZINESS IS
FAILING TO GO TO
GOOD EXTREMES

DO THAT WHICH
LETS YOU SENSE
GOD'S PLEASURE

GOD REVEALS ON A
"NEED TO KNOW"
BASIS

WORDS COME FROM
THE HEART, NOT
THE VOICE BOX

**Notes/Dates Used**

RECKLESS WORDS
PIERCE LIKE
A SWORD

ALL THAT HAPPENS
TO YOU CAN BRING
YOU TO GOD

FAILURE IS THE
PATH OF LEAST
PERSISTENCE

UNBELIEF IS
IMPATIENCE
WITH GOD'S TIMING

TROUBLE OFTEN
STARTS OUT
AS FUN

NO GOD, NO PEACE.
KNOW GOD,
KNOW PEACE

FAITH DOES NOT
INSIST GOD ANSWER
OUR QUESTIONS

**Notes/Dates Used**

BELIEVE THAT ALL
YOUR EXPERIENCES
MATTER

GOD WOULD BE
UNKIND TO ANSWER
ALL OUR PRAYERS

FAITH REFUSES TO
PANIC BECAUSE
GOD IS NEAR

WE WANT MORE AND
MORE, BUT GOD IS
MORE THAN ENOUGH

WORSHIP
IS LIKE
HUGGING GOD

LIVE FOR
SOMETHING BIGGER
THAN YOURSELF

GOD IS
ACTIVELY WORKING
IN YOUR DAY

**Notes/Dates Used**

FAITH MEANS
TRUSTING GOD
WITH YOURSELF


ARE WE
SELF-RELIANT OR
GOD-RELIANT?


INCLUDE GOD IN
YOUR PLANS.
YOU'RE IN HIS


FAILURE IS AN
OPPORTUNITY
TO BEGIN AGAIN


LIFE IS A SERIES
OF MYSTERIES
TO BE SOLVED


BEING PROUD OF
OUR FAITH IS A
CONTRADICTION


DON'T SWEAT
THE SMALL
STUFF

**Notes/Dates Used**

OUR INTERRUPTIONS
CAN BE GOD'S
ASSIGNMENTS


PATIENCE MEANS
TRUSTING GOD
FOR THE FUTURE


CAN GOD HELP
HIMSELF TO
YOUR LIFE?


IN GOD'S WAY AND
IN GOD'S TIME —
BE PATIENT


THE LORD HELPS
US FIND MEANING
IN OUR PAIN


KEEP THE MAIN
THING THE
MAIN THING


THE LORD IS
COMMITTED
TO YOU

**Notes/Dates Used**

GOD CALLS US TO
FAITHFULNESS,
NOT TO SUCCESS


PEOPLE DON'T FAIL.
THEY STOP
TRYING


GOD CAN MOVE
US FROM SINFUL
SELF-ABSORPTION


FEAR KNOCKED,
FAITH ANSWERED.
NO ONE WAS THERE


TO BE POOR IS NOT
TO LACK MONEY
BUT A DREAM


WE CAN'T TAKE
OUR GRUDGES
TO HEAVEN


IMPATIENCE IS A
FORM OF
UNBELIEF

**Notes/Dates Used**

FAITH COUNTS
ON GOD
TO HELP

DON'T GET IN
GOD'S WAY WHEN
HE GOES TO WORK

YOUR HARD TIMES
ARE NOT
POINTLESS

LAUGHTER IS
THE MUSIC OF
THE SOUL

GENEROSITY COSTS
LESS THAN
SELFISHNESS

GET OUTSIDE
YOURSELF SO GOD
CAN GET INTO YOU

NEVER BORROW
SORROW FROM
TOMORROW

**Notes/Dates Used**

OUR HEARTS ARE
RESTLESS UNTIL
THEY REST IN GOD


BEING WRONGED
IS NOT AS BAD
AS DOING WRONG


YOU CANNOT
GO WHERE
GOD IS NOT


GOD WILL GIVE US
POWER FOR WHAT
HE WANTS US TO DO


HOLD YOUR TEMPER
WHEN OTHERS
LOSE THEIRS


GUILT IS GOD'S
GENTLE HARSHNESS
SO HE CAN FORGIVE


THINGS MAY BE BAD
BUT REMEMBER,
GOD IS GOOD

**Notes/Dates Used**

SPIRITUAL SEEKERS
TAKE NOTE: GOD
IS SEEKING YOU


THE GOOD IS EVER
THE ENEMY OF
THE BEST


MAKE GOD
YOUR
PREOCCUPATION


NEVER
WASTE
YOUR PAIN


COURAGE IS FEAR
THAT HAS
SAID ITS PRAYERS


DO YOU KNOW
ANYONE WHO HAS
WON THE RAT RACE?


WHATEVER IS
DENIED CANNOT
BE HEALED

**Notes/Dates Used**

TREASURE GOD
MORE THAN
YOUR TREASURE


GOD YEARNS TO
MAKE YOUR
HEART HIS HOME


AIM TO MAKE YOUR
MAIN APPETITE A
HUNGER FOR GOD


DON'T GIVE UP
ON YOURSELF.
GOD HASN'T


KNEEL BEFORE GOD
AND YOU CAN STAND
BEFORE ANYTHING


WITH JESUS CHRIST
ALL OF LIFE
IS MANAGEABLE


TO BE FULL OF GOD
WE CAN'T BE
FULL OF SELF

**Notes/Dates Used**

HAPPY ARE THOSE
WHO GIVE
THEMSELVES TO GOD


GIVE UP HOPE
OF HAVING A
BETTER PAST


OUR
APPETITES DEFINE
US


THIS CHURCH IS
CHRIST'S CLINIC
FOR YOUR HEALING


IF YOU'RE THROUGH
GROWING,
YOU'RE THROUGH


IF YOU CHASE TWO
RABBITS,
BOTH WILL ESCAPE


GOD CAN TURN
YOUR SETBACK
INTO A COMEBACK

**Notes/Dates Used**

GOD CAN'T RESIST
PEOPLE WHO
ADMIT THEIR NEED


KNEE-MAIL
GOD TODAY —
PRAY


GIVE UP TO
GOD WHAT HAS
YOU DOWN


WHEN LIFE IS NOT
IDEAL, GOD CAN
BE MOST REAL


WITHOUT GOD WE
CANNOT. WITHOUT
US, GOD WILL NOT


DON'T LIVE
WAITING FOR YOUR
LIFE TO BEGIN


GOD DOESN'T GIVE
GUARANTEES, ONLY
OPPORTUNITIES

**Notes/Dates Used**

SWITCH YOUR
WORRY LIST TO
A PRAYER LIST


GOD GOES
WHERE
HE'S WANTED


FAILURE CAN BE
PARALYZING OR IT
CAN BE ENERGIZING


DON'T DO ALL YOU
COULD, JUST WHAT
YOU SHOULD


OUR INADEQUACY
CAN SHOW GOD TO
BE ADEQUATE


IF YOU WRESTLE
WITH GOD,
PRAY YOU LOSE


HANDLE FAILURE
SO AS
TO SUCCEED

**Notes/Dates Used**

OUR HURT
REACHES
GOD'S HEART

WE DON'T NEED TO
KNOW EVERYTHING
WE WANT TO KNOW

GOD
FORGIVES
GOOF UDS

IF GOD IS YOUR
CO-PILOT,
SWAP SEATS

NOTHING CAN
MAKE US HAPPIER
THAN GOD

THE BEST EXERCISE
IS WALKING
WITH THE LORD

WHEN DAZZLED BY
GOD, SIN CAN'T
EASILY SEDUCE

Notes/Dates Used

WORSHIP WITH US
AS WE TRY TO GET
A GRIP ON GOD

GOD IS HOLY AND
LOFTY, BUT
HE'S NOT ALOOF

THE BEST TRIP TO
TAKE IS MEETING
PEOPLE HALFWAY

PRIORITIZE PEOPLE
BY WHO WILL CRY
AT YOUR FUNERAL

THE ENJOYMENT OF
GOD IS THE
SUPREME PLEASURE

LET'S CARRY OUT
JUSTICE BUT NOT
GIVE IN TO RAGE

TOO MANY PEOPLE
HAVE ONLY A NEAR
LIFE EXPERIENCE

**Notes/Dates Used**

GIVE UP THE
RAT RACE FOR
GOD'S RACE

NOTHING RUINS
TRUTH LIKE
STRETCHING IT

HE WHO
ANGERS YOU
CONTROLS YOU

OPPORTUNITY LIES
IN THE MIDDLE
OF DIFFICULTY

WHEN IT'S OUT OF
YOUR HANDS, FOLD
THEM IN PRAYER

WE DON'T NEED
EVERYTHING
WE WANT

BE A
SOUL PROVIDER
FOR YOUR CHILD

**Notes/Dates Used**

TIME KEEPS
EVERYTHING FROM
HAPPENING AT ONCE

DISCONTENTMENT
IS THE MORTAL
ENEMY OF PEACE

HAVE A PAIN?
YOU DON'T
HAVE TO BE ONE

THINGS
THAT HURT US
INSTRUCT US

THE DUTY
OF LOVE
IS TO LISTEN

OUR WANTS
ALWAYS EXCEED
OUR NEEDS

SEE THE HOLY
IN THE
ORDINARY

**Notes/Dates Used**

LUCK IS
THE IDOL
OF THE IDLE


FAILURE ISN'T A
CRIME, BUT
AIMING LOW IS


EXPERTS
WERE ONCE
BEGINNERS


THIS IS THE DAY
THE LORD
HAS MADE


GOD CAN USE
ORDINARY
PEOPLE


ALL YOU
CAN DO
IS ENOUGH


MAKE
TODAY
COUNT

**Notes/Dates Used**

GOD HUGS
PEOPLE
THRU PEOPLE


BEFORE ALL
ELSE FAILS,
PRAY


JOIN
US
SUNDAY


GOD HAS
CHOSEN
YOU


SAY A
GOOD WORD
TODAY


EACH DAY
IS
A GIFT


YOU CAN
TRUST
GOD

**Notes/Dates Used**

DON'T FEAR —
GOD'S
NEAR


LIVE TODAY
AS IF IT'S
YOUR LAST


KEEP
GOSSIP
TOP SECRET


GOD IS
YOUR GREATEST
NEED


GOD
CARES
FOR YOU


STOP BY
FOR
GOOD WORSHIP


FAMILIARITY
CAN STIFLE
IMAGINATION

**Notes/Dates Used**

TALK
TO GOD
TODAY


LET US PRAY
FOR YOU
DIAL (your phone #)


DON'T PUT OFF
CONQUERING
PROCRASTINATION


CONTROL YOUR
TEMPER,
DON'T LOSE IT


THIS COULD
BE YOUR
CHURCH


YOUR KIDS
WOULD LOVE
SUNDAY SCHOOL


DRIVE BY TODAY,
STOP IN
ON SUNDAY

**Notes/Dates Used**

EVERY MOMENT
IS
IMPORTANT


WE'LL NEVER SAY,
"THERE'S NOTHING
MORE TO DO."


WE ARE ALL
INDEBTED
TO OTHERS


SMALL DEEDS
BEAT BIG
INTENTIONS


GOD TEACHES US
THROUGH
TROUBLES


WORSHIP IS
OUR GIFT
TO GOD


DON'T SPEND
TIME,
INVEST IT

**Notes/Dates Used**

TO HAVE
A FRIEND,
BE ONE

VISITORS
EXPECTED

PARENTHOOD —
TO HAVE
AND TO MOLD

GOD
IS
ENOUGH

PRAYER
IS A
LOCAL CALL

GOD WILL SUPPLY.
WE MUST
APPLY

THE ONLY
WAY OUT
IS THROUGH

                                                    Notes/Dates Used

FEELING DOWN?
LOOK
UP!


TO BE LOVED,
BE
LOVABLE


WE HAVE
A PEW
FOR YOU


WHO WE ARE IS
MORE IMPORTANT
THAN WHAT WE DO


OPPORTUNITIES
AND OBSTACLES
GO TOGETHER


HUMBLE TALENT
BEATS
IDLE GENIUS


TO SLEEP,
COUNT BLESSINGS,
NOT SHEEP

**Notes/Dates Used**

OUR GREATEST
NEED IS TO
PLEASE GOD

A HALF TRUTH
MAY BE THE
WRONG HALF

SOME OF OUR
"NEEDS" ARE
ONLY "WANTS"

TRUE
REFRESHMENT
SERVED HERE

LIFE ROCKY?
DEPEND ON
THE "ROCK"

TO BE
PLEASED,
PLEASE

THINGS MAY
BE BAD, BUT
GOD IS GOOD

**Notes/Dates Used**

GOD WHISPERS
IN PLEASURE AND
SHOUTS IN PAIN

ALWAYS BE
EMPLOYED
BY GOD

ARGUING WITH
GOD IS A
LOSING BATTLE

OUR GOD IS
WHATEVER
WE LOVE MOST

GOD ALWAYS
WALKS AHEAD
OF US

DON'T SUCCEED
AT THE
WRONG THING

TRY US.
WE'LL
LIKE YOU

**Notes/Dates Used**

TIME IS
ONE OF
GOD'S TOOLS

SUCCESS IS
GROWING THROUGH
FAILURE

UNBELIEF IS
IN THE HEART,
NOT THE MIND

TRUTH IS
EASIER TO FIND
THAN TO FACE

CROWD OUT
EVIL
WITH GOOD

ASK GOD TO
GIVE STRENGTH
FOR TODAY

TELL THE TRUTH
TO HELP,
NOT TO HURT

**Notes/Dates Used**

A USER-FRIENDLY CHURCH

DO WHAT YOU OUGHT, NOT JUST WHAT YOU WANT

LOVE OFTEN NEEDS BACKBONE

WORSE THAN SIN IS THE DENIAL OF SIN

GOD IS NOT RELUCTANT TO ANSWER PRAYER

GOD'S DELAYS ARE NOT DENIALS

GOD IS THE BEST FATHER

**Notes/Dates Used**

SWALLOW YOUR
PRIDE. IT'S NOT
FATTENING

GOD CAN FILL
THE CUP THAT'S
TURNED UP

LOVE DOES
AWAY WITH
ENEMIES

I-CENTERED
OR
GOD-CENTERED?

NOTHING
TEACHES LIKE
TROUBLES

VIEW LIFE
THROUGH THE
FILTER OF FAITH

YOU DON'T KNOW
YOUR POTENTIAL
UNTIL YOU TRY

**Notes/Dates Used**

OUR SPECIAL GUEST
ON SUNDAY
IS JESUS


LUCKY BREAKS
COME MOST TO
THE PREPARED


TO PRAY OR
NOT TO PRAY?
PRAY ANYWAY


HEAVEN —
DON'T MISS IT
FOR THE WORLD


HAPPY HOURS
ARE EACH
SUNDAY MORNING


BE A HUMAN
BEING, NOT JUST
A HUMAN DOING


DISAPPOINTMENTS
BECOME GOD'S
APPOINTMENTS

**Notes/Dates Used**

THE GREATEST
ABILITY IS
DEPENDABILITY

BAD ODDS DON'T
MATTER IF GOD
IS IN CONTROL

THE BEST
GIFT IS
YOURSELF

GOD WILL
SPEAK TO YOU
TODAY

GOD FORGETS
THE SINS
WE CONFESS

DON'T BUILD
WALLS. BUILD
BRIDGES

CHILDREN ARE
A GIFT.
HANDLE WITH LOVE

**Notes/Dates Used**

GOOD IS THE
FRUIT OF EFFORT,
NOT CHANCE


RESPOND TO LIFE,
DON'T JUST
REACT


ASK GOD TO
STAND BETWEEN YOU
AND YOUR TROUBLES


WHERE FAITH
GROWS,
FEAR FLEES


LIMITATIONS CAN
BE GOD'S WAY
TO GUIDE US


FAILURE CAN BE
A BETTER TEACHER
THAN SUCCESS


WITH PAST HURTS
WE CAN HELP
THOSE HURTING NOW

**Notes/Dates Used**

TROUBLES ARE
THE FRUITFUL SOIL
OF GROWTH

RESPECT GRAVITY
AND GOD'S
OTHER LAWS

TRUTH IS NOT
DETERMINED BY
A MAJORITY VOTE

LISTENING IS
THE BETTER PART
OF CONVERSATION

THERE'S NO RIGHT
WAY TO DO A
WRONG THING

WORRY GIVES
SMALL THINGS
BIG SHADOWS

ACHIEVERS
HAVE WILLS,
NOT WISHES

**Notes/Dates Used**

WE BREAK
WHEN WE BREAK
GOD'S WILL


MAKE GOD'S
PROVISION
YOUR SUPPLY


GOD'S PROMISES
ARE AS GOOD
AS FACTS


DON'T FOCUS ON
LACK OF LUCK
BUT ON THE LORD


MEASURE
TWICE,
CUT ONCE


GOD IS ALWAYS
MORE THAN
WE THINK HE IS


TIME CAN BE
LOST BUT NOT
RETRIEVED

**Notes/Dates Used**

EVIL DOES NOT
SURRENDER
WITHOUT A FIGHT


WITH OUR EYES
WE LOOK, BUT
DO WE SEE?


WITH OUR EARS
WE HEAR, BUT
DO WE LISTEN?


TOUGH PROBLEMS?
STRATEGIZE LESS
AND PRAY MORE


SIN IS HAVING
OUR OWN WAY
AND NOT GOD'S


CONVERSATION IS
MORE THAN TWO
MONOLOGUES


UNDER SAME
MANAGEMENT FOR
OVER 2,000 YEARS

**Notes/Dates Used**

DON'T FEEL
GOD NEAR?
HE IS ANYWAY


THE WORST
FAILURE IS
FAILING TO TRY


THE MIND IS
A GARDEN.
KEEP IT WEEDED


JUST FOR
TODAY ...
DON'T GIVE UP


GOD USES BROKEN
SOIL, CLOUDS,
BREAD ... & PEOPLE


WHAT DOESN'T
WORK OUT CAN BE
WORKED THROUGH


OUR WEAKNESS
AND GOD'S STRENGTH
GO WELL TOGETHER

Notes/Dates Used

PATIENCE
SHOWS
INTELLIGENCE

FACE A CLOSED
DOOR? LOOK FOR
AN OPEN WINDOW

GOD PROTECTS
IN STORMS,
NOT FROM STORMS

OUR CHURCH
IS PRAYER
CONDITIONED

WHAT GOD ASKS
OF YOU HE CAN DO
THROUGH YOU

FORCE OPEN A
ROSEBUD & YOU
RUIN THE FLOWER

GOD CREATED US
SO HE'D HAVE
SOMEONE TO LOVE

**Notes/Dates Used**

DON'T SEEK TO BE
SPECTACULAR,
JUST SPECIAL


INTERRUPTIONS
ARE UNEXPECTED
OPPORTUNITIES


BE CHILD-LIKE
BUT NOT
CHILDISH


RECOVERING
SINNERS
MEET HERE


DIFFICULTIES
ARE THE
FOOD OF FAITH


ANALYZE LESS
AND
NOTICE MORE


GOD WILL SEND
YOU A SECRET
MESSAGE TODAY

**Notes/Dates Used**

WE MAY BE GOD'S
ANSWER TO OUR
OWN PRAYER


SILENCE AND
SOLITUDE LET US
HEAR FROM GOD


HAVE A TOUGH MIND
AND A
TENDER HEART


THE DEMANDING
IS NOT ALWAYS
IMPORTANT


NO MOMENT
IS
TRIVIAL


TAKE BOTH PRAISE
AND BLAME
WITH SOME SALT


MORE & MORE
MAY NOT BE
BETTER & BETTER

**Notes/Dates Used**

DELIGHT IN
GOD
MOST OF ALL

GOD HAS
FAITH
IN YOU

TO BE CONTENT
IS
TO BE RICH

YOU DON'T HAVE
TO EARN
GOD'S FAVOR

EVERY ENDING
IS A NEW
BEGINNING

MOTIVE IS
AS IMPORTANT
AS MOTION

OUR HEARTS
HURT AND
NEED DR. JESUS

**Notes/Dates Used**

THIS CHURCH IS A
FRANCHISED
OUTLET OF GOD'S


WHATEVER ELSE
YOU WEAR,
WEAR A SMILE


LISTEN RATHER
THAN JUST WAITING
TO SPEAK


ONLY GET EVEN
WITH THOSE WHO
HAVE HELPED YOU


GOD HEARS THE
HEART AS MUCH
AS THE VOICE


SEEK GOD'S LOVE,
NOT THE NEED
TO BE NEEDED


YOUR GREATEST
ASSET IS
YOUR CHARACTER

|  | Notes/Dates Used |
|---|---|

MOVE A MOUNTAIN
BY STARTING WITH
A FEW STONES

THE GREATEST
PROOF FOR GOD IS
A CHANGED LIFE

ETERNITY MAKES
ALL PEOPLE
CONTEMPORARIES

PUT GOD AT THE
CENTER OF
YOUR WORLD

FORGIVENESS IS
THE ROAD FROM
A BAD PAST

AVOID TROUBLE IF
YOU CAN, FACE IT
IF YOU MUST

PRAYER CHANGES
THINGS BUT IT
ALSO CHANGES US

**Notes/Dates Used**

THE GOOD OL' DAYS
WEREN'T ALL
THAT GOOD

PAST ACTIONS COME
BACK TO HAUNT
OR BLESS US

MAKE AN
APPOINTMENT
WITH GOD TODAY

STRIVE TO
SEE YOURSELF
AS GOD DOES

CHOICE, NOT
CHANCE, GUIDES
OUR DESTINY

GOD DOES MORE
THAN WE CAN
UNDERSTAND

JOY IS A
BY-PRODUCT
OF TRUSTING GOD

**Notes/Dates Used**

TEMPTATION IS
BEST RESISTED
AT THE BEGINNING


IN EVERYTHING, WE
TRUST MORE THAN
WE UNDERSTAND


OUR POSSESSIONS
SHOULDN'T
POSSESS US


BE ORIGINAL.
DON'T MAKE THE
SAME MISTAKES


LIVE LIKE GOD
LOVES YOU,
BECAUSE HE DOES


GET YOURSELF
OUT OF THE WAY
TO LISTEN WELL


AS A TOOL IS
OF USE TO US,
SO WE ARE TO GOD

Notes/Dates Used

LIFE AGES SOME
PEOPLE AND
SEASONS OTHERS


SIN IS PLACING
OUR CHOICE BEFORE
THE RIGHT CHOICE


MORE KNOWLEDGE
WON'T OFFSET A
LACK OF WISDOM


ALL DESIRES
SHOULDN'T BE
SATISFIED


PEOPLE TOLERATE
A TALKER BUT
LOVE A LISTENER


YOUR LIFE'S A
STORY. WRITE
IT WELL


IF ALL BIBLES
DISAPPEARED WOULD
YOU MISS THEM?

**Notes/Dates Used**

DO YOUR BEST
AND LET
GOD DO THE REST


SPEAK SO AS
TO BENEFIT
THOSE WHO LISTEN


PRAYER CHANGES
OUR MINDS,
NOT GOD'S


EMPATHY IS
YOUR PAIN
IN MY HEART


GOD KNOWS
YOUR
LOAD LIMIT


VISION IS THE
ART OF SEEING
THE INVISIBLE


LET US HELP
YOUR CHILD GET
TO KNOW JESUS

**Notes/Dates Used**

ANGER IS JUST
ONE LETTER
SHORT OF DANGER


WE MISS 100%
OF THE SHOTS
WE NEVER TAKE


YOU CAN HAVE
A FRIENDSHIP
WITH JESUS


FAITH CAN ONLY
EXIST IN THE
FACE OF DOUBTS


WE MAY NOT KNOW
YOU, BUT WE COULD
IF YOU LET US


FAILURE CAN MAKE
A SUCCESSFUL
CHARACTER


WHAT HAS GOD
ENTRUSTED
TO YOUR CARE?

**Notes/Dates Used**

BELIEVE IN
YOURSELF.
GOD DOES

THE INNOCENT
HAVE NOTHING
TO DREAD

PRAYER LEADS
TO A
CALMPLEX

SIN IS
ITS OWN
PUNISHMENT

TREAT SUCCESS
AND FAILURE
MUCH THE SAME

KNOWING TRUTH
REQUIRES THAT
WE LIVE IT

PUT GOD AT
YOUR CENTER
AND BE BALANCED

**Notes/Dates Used**

LAUGHTER IS
WHAT FAITH
SOUNDS LIKE


SEE FAILURE
AS
FORCED GROWTH


GOD'S HELP MORE
THAN MATCHES
OUR NEED


CHRIST MAKES US
SUBJECT TO NONE,
SERVANT OF ALL


TODAY'S CHOICES
CREATE TOMORROW'S
REALITIES


WHAT DISTRACTS
YOU FROM
GOD?


"THY KINGDOM COME"
MEANS OUR
KINGDOM MUST GO

**Notes/Dates Used**

DO SOMETHING
IN WHICH
YOU RISK FAILURE

OWN YOUR
ACTIONS & OWN
UP TO THEM

OUR BUSYNESS
BLOCKS
GOD'S BUSINESS

FAITH MEANS TO
BELIEVE IN SPITE
OF DOUBTS

OUR WEAKNESS IS
NOT A BARRIER
TO GOD'S PURPOSES

LIFE IS
THE SUM OF
OUR DECISIONS

TO MOVE AHEAD,
FALL BACK
ON JESUS

**Notes/Dates Used**

LOVE THE WAY
YOU'D LIKE
TO BE LOVED

IF YOU THINK YOU
UNDERSTAND GOD,
THINK AGAIN

GOD'S GOODNESS
IS HIDDEN IN
OUR SUFFERING

WE WERE CREATED
FOR HAPPINESS.
IT'S FOUND IN GOD

GOD YEARNS
TO BRING US
HIS GOOD

WHEREVER
YOU ARE,
BE ALL THERE

NOTHING IS
A MYSTERY
TO GOD

**Notes/Dates Used**

WE HAVE A GOD-
SHAPED VACUUM
ONLY GOD CAN FILL

GOD COULD SAVE
YOU OR HIS SON,
BUT NOT BOTH

REMEMBER THE
ULTIMATE
GIFT-GIVER

GOD DOESN'T
ALWAYS CARE TO
EXPLAIN HIMSELF

WE DO NOT HAVE
TO SURRENDER TO
WRONG APPETITES

HISTORY
IS
HIS STORY

WE HAVE
GOD'S BEST AT
CHRIST'S EXPENSE

**Notes/Dates Used**

LIVE BEYOND
YOURSELF AND
GOD DRAWS NEAR

SIN THAT'S
FORGIVEN GIVES
US OUR SONG

A LOT OF KNEELING
WILL KEEP YOU
IN GOOD STANDING

HAVING TRUTH
DECAY? BRUSH UP
ON YOUR BIBLE

WISDOM IS HAVING
MUCH TO SAY AND
NOT SAYING IT

www.ingramcontent.com/pod-product-compliance
Lightning Source LLC
Chambersburg PA
CBHW071706040426
42446CB00011B/1942